Behavioural Safety for Leaders
By
Howard Lees and Bob Cummins

Behavioural Safety for Leaders is not intended to be an exhaustive text but an introduction of how to utilise behavioural science within the field of health and safety. It is the second edition of Hollin Books 'Behaviour Based Safety', re-titled to take into account that this edition is aimed at leaders, managers and safety professionals.

Other booklets published by Hollin books are:-
How to Escape from Cloud Cuckoo Land
Behavioural Coaching (second edition)
How to Empty the 'Too Hard' Box
Ideas for Wimps
Notes on Behavioural Management Techniques
The Too Busy Trap

GW00507568

Hollin Books
21 Ashbrook Rd
Bollington
Macclesfield
Cheshire
SK10 5LF
Hlees@hollinconsulting.co.uk
www.bmtfed.com

First published (as BBS) by Hollin books June 2008
Second edition published February 2011
Hollin books is a division of Hollin Consulting Ltd
© Copyright 2009 Hollin Consulting Ltd
ISBN 978-0-9563114-5-0

Testimony for Behavioural Safety for Leaders

From 2011 to 2013, we have reduced our reportable injuries from 26 down to 3. I believe that a significant part of this reduction has been due to the roll out of BMT for Safety and our staff's use of Behavioural Science to improve the way we work.

Peter Farrer, Chief Operating Officer, Scottish Water.

I believe that Behavioural Safety is one of the most powerful tools that leaders have today and effective implementation will not only improve safety but bring about considerable efficiencies within an organisation.

James Bertram Health, Safety and Resilience Manager.
Scottish Police Services Authority.

Lees and Cummins have produced an accessible and challenging booklet that will have not a few business leaders re-evaluating their approach to safety in the workplace. I was especially taken with their Safety Continuum and look forward to the day when customers and their advisers recognise that real safety is not to be confused with the virtual safety represented by paper systems, auditing and after-the-fact KPIs. I hope that the ideas expressed in this booklet will open industry leaders' eyes to the practical reality of a culturally safe future.

John Chipman, Quality Manager, Costain.

This whole behavioural approach has changed the way I manage safety beyond all recognition. Creating an environment to succeed before you try any specific actions is the key to unlocking all the good will that already exists within the company. I shudder when I look back at the way we used to just send out long winded messages by email and think we were leading our people.

Sue Hill, Property Services Manager, Gough Group, NZ.

"This booklet offers a forthright insight into the true meaning of Safety Leadership. The no-nonsense approach to the issues covered makes it essential reading for Business Leaders who have the courage to challenge their own management style and the way Safety is currently managed within their own business. The notion that Safety is a value not a priority underpins the whole approach to establishing the correct environment whereby safety improvements are effected proactively."

Craig Reade, Project Manager, Costain.

Behavioural Safety for Leaders
By
Howard Lees and Bob Cummins

Behavioural Safety for Leaders

The cover photograph taken by Jean Lees is Shag Rock in Sumner, near Christchurch, New Zealand. A 7.1 magnitude earthquake struck at 4:35 am on 4 September 2010. A piece of Shag rock fell off. Since the 4th of September there have been some 4800 aftershocks.

On Boxing Day there was a 4.6 magnitude shock at 2.32am which brought down a number of shops in Cashel St, Christchurch. We have spent a lot of time in Christchurch and have an affinity with the city. We were shopping in Cashel St a few days before the earthquake. These two destructive earthquakes occurred early in the morning; miraculously no-one was killed.

On Tuesday 22nd February an earthquake hit Christchurch at lunch time, many people have been killed. This booklet is dedicated to the memory of the people who lost their lives and their families.

Bob and Howard would like to thank Joanne Lees for the excellent cartoons. Also our thanks go to Rachel Edwards, Nicole Gravina, Allison Reynolds, John Chipman and John Austin for the invaluable feedback on the text. Special thanks to Jean Lees, Nora Lees and Lynn Dunlop for editing this booklet.

Contents

Preface

Standing in court that day made it all the more real. Not that it wasn't real before, after all, we had been to his funeral, we had seen the anger in his son's eyes and heard the sobs from his wife. There we were, the Site Manager and I. It was 1998 and we were giving evidence at the Coroner's Court. The fatality had occurred on a construction site during our watch.

We had been carrying out an inspection of the site; a building of steel beams and columns with metal decking floors. We noticed a platform and ladder perched across the beams. This obviously (surely it was obvious to everyone) unsafe arrangement was not the agreed method of work. We spoke to the supervisor in charge and asked him to 'sort it out'. He promised us that he would deal with it straight away.

On the 2nd April 1998, 2 days after our discussion with the supervisor, two workers fell from the unsafe platform; one of the men died from his injuries.

Once you have experienced a fatality, you never forget it, you never want to forget it and you never stop asking – could I have done more? Was my action enough? Should I have relied upon a simple verbal transaction? Should I have relied upon the 'writing down' of a fatally unsafe piece of equipment on an inspection form? Looking back, knowledge of behavioural science would have helped me; it certainly has since I started studying it.

Bob Cummins

1.1 Introduction

At first glance safety performance is like any other area of business performance: it is a function of its environment. However, safety related behaviour needs to be more consistent and accurate. A business will continue to function with countless minor errors in spreadsheets or missed appointments, but with regard to safety, small variations in behaviour can lead to incidents and injury.

> " objectivity is at the core of behavioural science. "

The angle at which a Stihl saw is held can make the difference between a safe cut and an exploding blade. An offhand comment from a Director can lead to an unsafe working environment, days, even months after the comment was made.

It must be stressed that Behavioural Safety for Leaders is not a replacement for current safety processes; it is a valuable tool that leaders and managers can use to help improve safe conditions for workers by increasing the chances of making sustainable improvements to safety, using behavioural science as the catalyst.

Behavioural science is the science of human behaviour; it is founded on using data and analysis to come to conclusions about what is happening in the interactions of people. Objectivity is at the core of behavioural science.

Psychology seeks to understand what is going on inside the mind, to modify these internal phenomena and in doing so achieve behaviour change. Behavioural science observes the behaviour, seeks to modify the external environment and in doing so achieve behaviour change. Behavioural science sees each person as an individual who desires a totally unique set of reinforcers from their environment (their world).

Both mainstream psychology and behavioural science are used in seeking behaviour change. Critically, behavioural science has a greater verifiable record of achieving this and is also far easier for people to learn and apply.

A number of scientific terms are used in this booklet, simply described here: -

Antecedents

An antecedent is a request or prompt, something which is attempting to drive a particular behaviour. A sign that says 'don't smoke', a speed sign, or an email detailing how you will deliver a project are all antecedents. Antecedents are quite poor at driving behaviour if they are not paired with consequences. Examples of antecedents are emails, letters, safety notices, requests for attendance at meetings, phone messages, the law, company procedures etc.

Consequences

Consequences have the greatest impact on our behaviour. What happens to us following our behaviour will affect the likelihood of us performing the same behaviour again under similar circumstances.

Behavioural science states that there are two main consequence types that result in a behaviour occurring/recurring or stopping, they are defined as Reinforcement and Punishment.

Environment

The definition of environment here is the immediate location of the person, be it in their office, living room, their car - wherever the behaviour is occurring. A person's behaviour is mostly driven by the consequences that follow the behaviour. The environment will dictate the consequences you experience and this of course includes the other people in the room, office etc. Small changes in environment can result in significant changes in the behaviour of an individual.
The environment affects us and we affect the environment.

Example: Imagine an office full of people. Take one person out of the office and replace them with a different person. The environment has changed. The change could be very significant depending on who left and who came in.

Pinpointing

Pinpointing is the process used to make sure a behaviour is described accurately. Something is pinpointed when it complies with the following rules: -

1. **It can be seen or heard.**
2. **It can be measured, counted etc.**
3. **Two people would always agree that the behaviour occurred or not.**
4. **It is active (something is occurring).**

People who learn pinpointing can quickly develop skills which reduce the amount of assumption in their environment. This reduction of (sometimes destructive) assumptions increases the amount of informed comment, decisions and discussions.

It is advisable to gather data on situations via observations and keep notes of who actually said/did what. This significantly reduces the chance of unnecessary conflict created by assumption.

Research on use of email says that there is a 40% chance you will not read an email in the voice that was intended. This means that if you are already prejudiced against someone then the chance of you reading the email in the intended voice is nearly zero.

Pinpointing is a very useful skill for business. Next time someone relates something to you, if you are unsure of the message you can say, "can you pinpoint that for me please?"

> " Anything that requires mastery requires repetition. "

Shaping

Shaping is a simple concept which is very difficult to master.
It recognises that you can't get from step 1 to step 10 in one vertical stride. You sometimes have to first write out steps 2 through 9 and then carry them all out, one step at a time.

People sometimes ask, "I want to say this to my boss." Before you say anything you need to predict the chances of it being received the right way by your boss. "Not very good," will be the reply. Unfortunately, you have to shape to the goal you want to achieve, and this usually means a time-consuming set of steps which will shape the environment so that you can actually say what you want to say.

Shaping is not for the impatient, and a realisation that patience is the key can take some people some time. Many very reinforcing tools we use these days do not help to assist a patient approach e.g. email and voice mail. It is reinforcing working through a list of tasks, ticking actions off as you go. It is not naturally reinforcing taking the extra time to consider - Is this the right thing to say? Does something else have to be achieved before I can say this and get what I want?

Shaping is inherent in everything we learn; if you want to play an instrument, you repeat and repeat until you can play the tune. Anything that requires mastery requires repetition. Putting a group of employees to work effectively and safely requires a leader to choose carefully who will work with whom. It requires trial and error to find the best combinations. Iteration is trying things out and seeing what the result is, adjusting and trying again. This is shaping; it works. It's the only thing that does work when building a team.

1.2 How can you use behavioural science?

The key to sustaining long term improvement is to apply behavioural science to your business. Using behavioural science to improve your business requires people to understand the principles of the science but, most importantly, practise as they learn the subject. All staff must feel 'safe' and free from threat if they are to try new things and learn effectively.

> Once behavioural science techniques have been learned, they should be applied to your current procedures and behaviours in use within the company.

Learning how to use behavioural science with safety is a requirement for everyone in the business if safety performance is to be genuinely improved. There are many examples where behavioural science has achieved just that. Some major companies have not had an injury or incident for many years.

Once behavioural science techniques have been learned, they should be applied to your current procedures and behaviours in use within the company. Systems and processes should be reviewed and removed or altered if they do not produce the correct consequences to drive behaviour.

All current behaviours are driven by the local environment the performers find themselves in (e.g. an office or a work site). In other words, behaviours are shaped by what goes on in the environment. Primarily, there are reinforcers and punishers that are driving day to day behaviours and these consequences are the key to producing safe or unsafe performance.

1.3 Why apply behavioural science to safety?

1. We want to achieve better safety performance in the future.
2. If we carry on doing the same things, we will not see change.
3. We have done well so far but have reached a plateau in reducing injuries and incidents.
4. We feel OK but inefficient and sometimes bureaucratic in our processes.
5. What does our data say about our current systems and procedures?
6. Are we really taking into account that most safety issues are behaviour related?
7. What could we now do differently, and which measures would prove we have achieved genuine improvements?

Spreading the knowledge of behavioural science to people in a company produces a permanent change within the company. People better understand the downstream impact of their own behaviour and that of others. This knowledge, combined with new slim safety processes which recognise what's really important will create an improvement in the current safety and general workplace behaviours.

1.4 Safety terminology

Safety terminology should reflect the belief behind creating a safe place for people to work. The use of the word "accident" for example can create a feeling that the injury sustained was unavoidable.

Here is a short list of changes that will not only make much more sense but will help improve the way Health and Safety is perceived and thought of within your business.

> " To succeed, zero injuries needs to be a vision not a numbers game. "

Injury and incident, NOT accident

An accident is something that can't be controlled; genuine accidents in the safety field are rare events. Most injuries and incidents are in situations which are planned and involve humans behaving. Human behaviour is the primary contributory factor in almost all incidents and injuries.

Zero is a vision, NOT a goal

Stating that zero injuries is a goal is just a millstone around everyone's neck. Sometimes people pay themselves bonuses to achieve various states of zero injury; this shows a lack of understanding that the goal here is to create a safe place for people to work. Once the threat of someone losing a bonus comes into play then all kinds of avoidance behaviours ensue.

Safety is a value, NOT a priority

Safety cannot be a priority, it must be a value, and it must be the foundation on which everything else is based. Saying it's a priority goes against all the day to day data which says lots of other things are talked about more. Priorities change, Values remain.

An Injury is a chance to learn, NOT punish

There appears to be an increase in completely out of proportion responses when an injury or incident occurs. It could be predicated on the 'bonus for safety' culture which exists in some places. It always makes the future less safe rather than more safe. Management behaviours which deliver punishing consequences post-injury creates all kinds of future avoidance behaviour from the very people that need to be more open about what is happening in the workplace. If you 'blow up' when you get bad news, people will not tell you bad news. Opportunity missed!

1.5 Setting the local environment

It is easy to assume that the live site environment is where we should put our attention to improve safety. In fact what happens here is just a reflection of the general safety culture within the organisation. It is in the offices where the work is planned that the 'on site' environments are created.

It is more difficult to observe unsafe behaviours in the offices where the decisions are made regarding safety matters on existing or future facilities and sites. This is why it is paramount to roll out behavioural safety to the decision makers and the managers.

The project managers and supervisors are working within local environments, either tuned to behavioural safety or not, as a result of their senior manager's actions. It is the middle leaders that are the key to rolling out the behavioural safety education. The legacy of unsafe behaviour in the offices is played out in the site environment.

There is a significant difference between what people commonly predict will happen in regards to safety performance and what the science of behaviour says will actually happen. This difference is worth highlighting and it's worth doing before anything is cascaded.

Observation and measurement are the tools that will provide the opportunity for the adjustment of expectations. It is quite easy to solicit examples of company processes which are not adhered to. It is also quite easy to solicit examples of supervisors that deliver the right environment and examples of those that don't. The key here is to spread the behavioural knowledge and then follow the people who put the new learning into practice. They, in time, will bring along everyone else.

> " It is the creation of safe verbal behaviour in the upper levels of a company that creates the long-term safe working environments on sites. "

Ultimately, the key behaviours in creating a safe working environment are the verbal exchanges between the management and supervisors, and the supervisors and the workforce. It is the creation of safe verbal behaviour in the upper levels of a company that creates the long-term safe working environments on sites.

The opportunity to have these conversations is frequent; whether or not it happens is contingent on the relationships of the people involved. Managers and supervisors alike will need to develop robust relationships with each other and the workforce in order for safe places of work to be created. Someone has to make this clear and create an environment for it to thrive; this is the leader's role. Do not micromanage (break the chain), no matter how tempting, create the environment where everyone is doing their own job effectively.

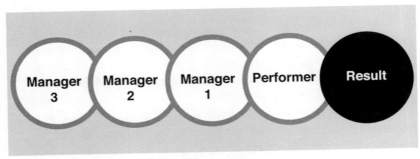

Consequence chain - don't break the chain

1.6 Your behaviour

Many people have stated that as they learn about behavioural science they are becoming more conscious of their own behaviour. The process of pinpointing a behaviour and observing the impact on others is very powerful in making us aware of how sensitive we are to what was said, who said it and how we responded.

We will find that we respond differently depending on who is doing the talking. Typically, we think that we have a set of personal values that we are consistent with, but this turns out not to be true.

If you say to someone, *"I'll ring you back after lunch"* and then you don't, what impact will this have on the person concerned? If it happens frequently will they distrust you? It seems a minor infraction but consider how you would feel and what you would do if someone consistently did this to you. Look at these events from the point of view of both parties; this is a valuable lesson. It's good to practise seeing situations from the performer's point of view, it can explain to you what's behind many mysterious situations.

It is very common to hear a boss say that, *"safety is paramount."* It is also very common that their own behaviour (what they do and say) does not support this statement. How many people actually point out the discrepancy to the boss? Potential consequences in the environment of bosses are usually pretty scary for most people, and so even though people will hear something they disagree with, they often say nothing to point it out. In reality, bosses tend to be oblivious to these opinions. But if they don't get any feedback, how can they be aware of this problem?

> " High levels of trust require high levels of honest feedback. "

Being conscious that you are not delivering honest feedback is part of the overall problem. Success thrives on honest feedback, and without it decisions are made that can make situations worse. High levels of trust require high levels of honest feedback. Some bosses find it difficult to embark on the behavioural safety journey as they do not like receiving honest feedback. Often they have conditioned themselves to live in a convenient happy bubble. Starting to say things you didn't say before is a matter of self management. Yes, it requires nerve, and it's very hard. But it's worth it.

1.7 How do I say what's on my mind?

> " When your confidence is high you will find you are much happier delivering feedback. "

The best thing to do is to pinpoint a behaviour you want to deliver feedback on. Consider a range of things you could say and pick something you are comfortable with. Pick the right time and the place to do it. Deliver your message. Look for a reaction.

Most of the time our fears about how someone will react to something we say are unfounded. We tend to operate on a very low threshold of where we think something will be confrontational.

You can experiment by trying out saying different things erring on the safe side. When your confidence is high you will find you are much happier delivering feedback, you will feel good about it. This is shaping. Patience is the key here.

1.8 How to do something different

If you really care about providing a safe place for people to work in, then start at a strategic level and look at what's happening right now. You are likely to find lots of safety rules, lots of process, lots of 'permission to proceed' type paperwork. This places the performers under threat of punishment ('do this or else'), and we know from behavioural science that people don't perform well in aversive environments.

Once you have studied the basics you can carefully observe the key behaviours that are causing dysfunction. These are likely to be verbal behaviours. It's important to get into the habit of writing these down, to make a note of when something is promised and to record whether it was delivered on time.

Observe decision making in the choice of suppliers and subcontractors and note anything inconsistent with safe delivery. Observe what happens after an incident or injury and analyse whether the subsequent actions by others will create a sustainable safer site in the future.

Front line workers are the best source of data on 'at risk' or 'safe behaviour', yet often, this source remains relatively untapped.

How could you better use this source of information?
Surveys – Asking a worker or member of staff directly to tell you what is wrong will often result in a false or censored response. We frequently carry out surveys using PowerPoint and anonymous voting buttons. Recognise that your workforce may be superstitious and untrusting; we have techniques which will minimise this. There may also be problems with literacy that you will have to take into account.

Observations – A number of behavioural programmes advocate the use of 'observation techniques', a programme of observing safe worker behaviours and feeding back to the workforce then monitoring improvement. This is mostly effective when carried out by fellow workers but involves creating the right environment i.e. free from threat and punishment. It also requires continual effort and support from managers and supervisors.

> Unsafe activity will occur where the performer feels in some way obliged to perform an unsafe or risky action.

In facilities or on sites it is easy to make observations of activities as there is physical work going on. This is where the behaviours within the local environments manifest themselves. Conducting observations here is the litmus test of the verbal behaviours which originally created the site environment.

If you see consistent safe behaviour, consistent adherence to PPE, consistent site tidiness, there is a good chance the existing data reflects this also, both incident data and audit data. The next step in data collection is 'observation' data.

1. **Make some behavioural observations in the work place.**
2. **Write down your data/measures and look for patterns, consistency etc.**
3. **Present your findings (in simple graphic form).**
4. **Set a new expectation and repeat the process.**
5. **Provide feedback to all the performers.**

Explaining to a worker that they may get injured if they don't work in a certain way is not enough to ensure safe working. Even when people are given full knowledge of the potential consequences they may still take risks. The obligation to work safely derives from either supervisor or peer pressure (the environment).

It is crucial to the process that once you have obtained data, whether it shows a good or bad picture that you feedback your information to the audience and discuss an appropriate action plan.

1.9 The real dangers of too much paperwork; Safety bulletins.

Safety bulletins are often relied upon to communicate requirements to prevent the reoccurrence of an accident. They rarely work; they are often not communicated properly and even if they were, they are an antecedent at best, and antecedents are only likely to be 20% effective.

You may observe the distribution of safety bulletins from 'corporate' following incidents that are similar to this one:

"Urgent notice to all staff, don't stick a pencil in your eye, it hurts, it can blind you, it will also make our safety statistics look worse, if anyone is caught sticking a pencil in their eye they will be dismissed."

These kinds of bulletins provide a smoke screen for the really important bulletins, and people can become desensitised from reading masses of bulletins. After a while, they read none of the bulletins presented to them.

Ask yourself if you really believe this piece of paper will actually change the way people work, if not, find a better way.

Understanding behaviour means understanding that you can detect the threshold at which point people can't take in any more safety materials. Testing to see if people are actually reading is paramount if you are distributing written material, 'spray and pray' is not an effective way of communicating information.

This excellent paper on safety communication is worth a read:-
You Know Safety But Admit It.....
You Don't Know Communication
Dr TJ Larkin & Sandar Larkin - www.larkin.biz

1.10 Subcontractors and suppliers

Subcontractors and suppliers must be chosen on actual safety performance. They should not be chosen simply on the basis of lowest cost with a token self assessment safety declaration.

It is easy to set up supply chain agreements and also easy to make them contingent on safe performance. It is also advisable to make suppliers and subcontractors take part in your behavioural safety process; after all, they are an extension of you, your workforce and your business

Safety as a value transcends all involved in projects and business. A full understanding of behavioural safety across all parties will ensure safety performance improvements are sustainable.

1.11 Measuring Health and Safety

> " There is a lot of luck involved in the avoidance of injuries. "

It is common, within the majority of industries, to measure injuries, incidents and close calls.

The number of injuries and incidents in some companies are at such a low level that it renders the data statistically irrelevant. A move to measuring lead indicators as the primary measure is the only way you can collect useful data that you can use to improve the environment. Even those who have successfully captured close call reporting are still measuring lag indicators.

Let's say your construction business of 560 employees has worked 672,000 hours in the last year and managed a 6 month long stint with no reportables, no minor injuries and a couple of close calls. Pretty good performance you may say, and you would be right. Your perception, however, is purely based on a lack of information; it is not based on any evidence of the effectiveness to create a safe environment.

If your company's main strategy for providing a safe environment is:–

- A competent workforce.
- A strong supervisory presence.
- Suitable premises/welfare/site set up/ material management.
- Availability of the appropriate tools.
- Appropriate systems and use of systems.

Then this is what you should measure. These are the lead indicators you may choose specifically for your site, company or environment.

Measure what keeps your business and your workers safe. Of course there is still a need to monitor injuries and close calls as long as you accept that these are lag indicators and not a measure of the creation of a safe environment.

What is a Close Call? A close call is an event that took place, i.e. no one slipped on the banana skin but the banana skin was still left on the floor. Unsafe conditions were created and could be observed by someone, noted and acted upon.

A close call is an unplanned event that did not result in injury, illness, or damage - but had the potential to do so. Examples of close calls could include someone tripping and almost falling down the stairs but managing to grab the handrail just in time, or when someone is almost hit by a reversing lorry. In these two examples, no injury resulted but this was the result of good luck rather than good management.

Why are Close Calls Important?
In the simple examples given above, if an injury had resulted, most organisations would have carried out an investigation into the circumstances and would have taken some form of corrective action. In other words, the decision to investigate and take corrective action is based on whether a person has been injured or not. Therefore, if no injury occurs, no investigation takes place and no attempt is made to prevent the same event occurring at some time in the future.

Does every close call need to be investigated? No, the exact action taken after a close call occurs depends upon the nature of the close call and the safety procedure. There is a balance between sensibly assessing which close calls to investigate and being exposed to too much data.

What are the uses of close call reporting? Close call reporting should be used at a site level to help spot and manage hazards on site by the workforce. For example, the worker experiences or witnesses a close call; this is reported to the supervisor, the supervisor corrects where possible the situation that lead to the close call. This is the primary objective of reporting close calls – to spot local hazards and control them, preventing them from happening again. The other objective of close call reporting is to highlight trends that may not have been previously identified and introduce preventative measures before any harm is caused.

The following points are examples of how to create a good and bad environment for close call reporting.

How to increase close call reporting

- Praise the worker for reporting the close call.
- See the reporting of a close call as a gift.
- Skilfully explain why you want the worker to report close calls and provide examples.
- Client and Contractor create a "safe non-threatening environment" for reporting close calls, i.e. a no blame culture.
- Provide feedback on a regular basis of the number of close calls reported.
- Provide feedback on a regular basis of improvements made from the reporting of close calls.
- Client to praise/ reward the contractor on creating a good close call reporting culture.
- Let the contractor action the findings from the close calls.
- Agree targets for close call reporting and measure actual vs desired.

In summary, increase close call reporting by – Making it an agreeable and worthwhile experience by praising / rewarding the workers for reporting close calls.
Use Positive Reinforcement.

How to decrease close call reporting

- Blame the person reporting the close call for the close call.
- Shout and bawl at the person for reporting the close call.
- Make the reporting of a close call difficult, i.e. filling out forms with names.
- Ask for a report on the close call.
- Worker / Contractor knowing that every close call would go past the director's desk.
- Contractor knowing that every close call would go to the client.
- Contractor believing that the Client will create more work for the contractor when a close call is reported.
- Take no notice when a worker reports a close call.
- Give no feedback to the workforce about improvements made as a result of close calls.
- Give no reason to the workforce for reporting close calls.
- Give no feedback to the workforce about number of close calls reported.
- Client gives no positive feedback or recognition to contractor for reporting close call.

In summary, stop close call reporting by – Punishing the person/company reporting the close call by creating more work for them, questioning them, bollocking them or ignoring them.
Use Punishment and Extinction.

1.12 Measuring something different

> " Every service that is avoided successfully
> is an opportunity to reinforce the
> behaviour that lead to that avoidance. "

Here is an example of how you can change the focus and improve performance just by choosing to measure something different.

Most construction companies measure the damage caused to utility services such as power, water, gas, street lighting etc. whether it is by frequency rate or by service struck. It is also quite easy to put a cost to such damage as inevitably, someone has to repair the service. What is not measured however is the number of services that have been painstakingly avoided, protected and remain unscathed during the excavation operation.

If you only measure how many services have been damaged and do not compare it to the number that have been avoided, you cannot fully appraise the performance of your workers or recognise proportional and representative improvement. The lack of service strikes may simply be because there are no services to hit.

Every service that is avoided successfully is an opportunity to reinforce the behaviour that lead to that avoidance. If you are not measuring the successfully avoided services you are certainly not reinforcing the behaviour you actually want to see more of.

Next time you have a workforce excavating through a jungle of services, measure the amount of services avoided on a regular basis, compare this to the amount of services struck and discuss with your workers how they avoided these. Make sure you feedback and display the results. You will soon find that performance improves.

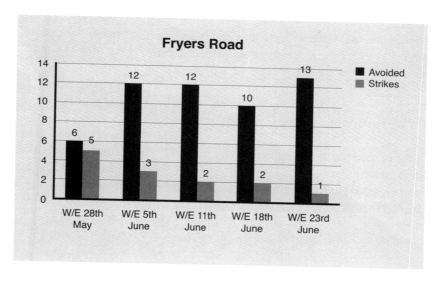

1.13 New worker arrives on site

Any new worker to a construction site will hear the top-level safety message at induction. He will then walk out onto site and be able to observe whether the site culture indicated at induction is real. He will look around, and if he sees inconsistency, he will feel a little insecure about what to do. He will certainly not want to get in trouble with, or be teased by either the foreman or his work colleagues. Peer pressure and supervisor pressure will prevail; he will want to 'fit in'.

The example above is the key moment of the behavioural process: Do we mean what we say?

If the picture painted at induction was true and safety behaviours are accepted as a value to everyone involved, then the chances of this worker behaving safely after entering the site is high. If the picture painted was false, then the chances that he will do so are greatly reduced.

> " Training without coaching has little effect. "

The competency of a new worker on site is critical to safety performance. The agreement of when a new worker is classed as 'Competent' is often debated amongst safety bodies including the HSE and IOSH. It is accepted that instruction and training alone is not sufficient. The HSE's Approved Code of Practice for CDM suggests that it can take up to 2 years for a new worker to become competent and only if they undertake a programme of continued development.

Research shows that information dissemination and training alone is an ineffective implementation method. Consultation and training combined are more effective than training alone and training alone is more effective than simply providing manuals or statements that describe what has to be done.

Training workshops have little impact on practice but when coupled with coaching can contribute greatly to an individual's competence.

Ensuring that the workforce and staff are competent extends far beyond the checking they have the right cards or putting them on a training course. Training without coaching has little effect; therefore to ensure a competent workforce you need to have a program of purposeful, directed coaching and support.

1.14 The Safety Continuum – 5 Stages of a safety culture

There are a number of different definitions of a safety culture. Cox and Cox described it as: *a term often used to describe the way in which safety is managed in the workplace, and often reflects "the attitudes, beliefs, perceptions and values that employees share in relation to safety"* (Cox and Cox, 1991). The ACSNI describe it as: *the product of individual and group values, attitudes, perceptions, competencies and patterns of behaviour.......* (Advisory Committee on Safety of Nuclear Installations 1993).

These are simple subjective ways of describing a safety culture; however there is still a need to measure the safety culture.

It is essential to have an understanding of what good practice looks like. By visualising what good practice looks like, whether through experience or through belief, you should be able to describe the attributes and characteristics of a model culture.

What pinpointed behaviours would you expect to observe within the environment of a model safety culture? What behaviour would you expect from your worker if faced with having to use a piece of equipment that was not suitable for the job? What reaction would you expect from your director when you informed him of a safety incident? What do you wish your safety procedures looked like (quantity and quality)?

If you can imagine all these specifics, you can describe to others what good practice looks like. You can start to measure where you are against your vision but more importantly you can create a shaping plan to get you from where you are to where you want to be.

The Safety Continuum is a measuring tool developed by the BMT Federation. It helps to identify different cultural stages. There are 5 in total, ranging from poor to great. By using behaviours to describe the stages in a culture, it is possible to map your own company's culture. The mapping process not only allows you to recognise your current behaviours, it also helps to identify the behaviours you should exhibit to get you to the next stage.

The 5 stages of a safety culture

Clueless	Negligent	Compliant	Getting There	Gold Standard
Safety is not considered	Safety is avoided	Safety is a distraction	Safety is a priority	Safety is a value

- Moving from 'Clueless' to 'Negligent' may happen automatically as a company grows from conception.
- Making the transition from 'Negligent' to 'Compliant' requires effort and usually pressure from external business or enforcement bodies.
- Improving from 'Compliant' to 'Getting There' requires internal conviction and a willingness to improve; scepticism may still exist in parts of the organisation.
- Getting to the final 'Gold Standard' stage of the evolutionary culture scale requires recognition that Safety is a Value and that it will only be successful if behavioural science is used to predict and manage behaviour.

The 5 stages in summary

CLUELESS – Safety is not considered
- At best hiring an external safety consultant to carry out the bare legal requirements.
- Safety rules only appear in paperwork or posters.
- Some signs on site.
- No records of injuries or incidents.
- No tool box talks or start briefings.
- No director named responsible for safety.
- No 'in house' safety advisor.

NEGLIGENT – Safety is avoided
- Turning a blind eye when there is knowledge of hazards or ignoring legal requirements.
- External safety consultant to provide standard paperwork, notices, signs etc.
- Taking risks to save short term money.
- Running the business with the knowledge of safety non-compliance and breaches.
- Punishing of people who report safety breaches or hazards.
- Content with having guilty knowledge.
- Illegal activity.

COMPLIANT – Safety is a distraction
- "We haven't killed anyone, we must be successful."
- Procedures and processes in place, customised where necessary.
- 'In house' safety advisor.
- More virtual safety than real safety.
- Safety advisors as policemen.
- Safety is on the agenda.
- Recording RIDDORS and other injuries reported.
- Seeking safety awards.
- Procurement involvement is just a safety questionnaire.

- Sub contractors' injuries and incidents not part of overall statistics.
- Minor incidents and close calls not reported.
- Still using old language - accidents, near misses.
- Still using only lag indicators.
- No culture surveys.
- No training for foremen on start of shift briefings or tool box talks.
- Safety is the job of the safety department.
- Blame culture / arse covering. Director named responsible for safety (also QA, environment and HR, perhaps).

GETTING THERE – Safety is a priority
- Safety culture surveys.
- Safety strategy required by client and developed and delivered by contractor.
- Safety Director.
- Audits include behavioural elements.
- Behavioural training programme.
- Foremen get trained and measured on tool box talks and START briefings, and communications.
- Lean safety tools.
- Safety Advisors as coaches.
- Adopting new language of incidents and close calls.
- Close calls and minors being recorded and trended.
- Have a mixture of lagging and leading indicators.
- No longer seeking awards.
- Not yet trusting people to do the right thing.
- Visiting contractor's other sites before procuring (verifying).
- Only one set of safety statistics which includes sub contractors.
- Basic PPE always in evidence; hats, vests and boots.
- Blanket policies in place on items such as safety glasses, gloves and mobile phones.
- Lots of meaningless data being collected.

GOLD STANDARD – Safety is a value
- Predictive safety KPIs.
- No specific Safety Director on the board.
- Lean safety department.
- People regularly using the ABC model.

- Behavioural techniques rolled out to all staff.
- Project delivery (operational) people investigate incidents and injuries and write safety procedures.
- Meaningful data.
- Using new technology to increase surety of process (i.e. Tool hound, HAV metre).
- Sophisticated supply chain.
- Performance management of contractors.
- Safety standards dictated by individual work group.
- Environment designed to create safe working.
- Peer to peer challenge on safety infringements.
- Method statements are lean and written by work group.
- Mindful fluency.
- Frequently hear 'How is this decision going to affect safety?'
- Dynamic risk assessments.
- Seeking dissenting opinions often witnessed.
- Evidence based improvement plans.
- Zero injuries and incidents.
- No bonuses paid for safety.
- You can measure the multiplier effect of behavioural safety on profits.
- Significantly superior than competitors on relationships, planning and prediction.
- Sustainable business practices with clients and supply chain.
- Feedback rich environment.
- Frequent testing for risk.
- Leadership is self aware.
- Site looks and feels right.

1.15 Applying behavioural safety to what you do already

> Adopting behavioural science means that you test and amend your processes and procedures.

Hopefully, you will by now have realised that using behavioural science to improve safety does not mean that you abandon your already established and embedded procedures. Adopting behavioural science means that you test and amend your processes and procedures with the knowledge you now have to ensure that they are behaviourally sound, in that they will create either the desired environment or the desired behaviour using Antecedents and Consequences.

Test the current processes that you believe should be making a difference. Ask, "what is the purpose of this process?" Having established the objective, does your process identify the pinpointed behaviours that will then meet the objective?

Here are 10 faults common to processes in business developed without using behavioural science.

Procedures
- Pinpointed behaviours not identified, or
- Procedures not tested and punishes the user, or
- Is often disjointed from reality.

Near Miss/Close Call Reporting
- Workers perceived that they are ignored due to lack of feedback, or
- Reported close calls generate more work and punishes those reporting them.

Site Inspections
- Sites/workplaces being inspected can never achieve 100%, or
- Inspection doesn't identify behaviours either at risk or safe.

Worker Consultation
- Environment for honest feedback does not exist, or
- The real elephants in the room are ignored and not dealt with.

Safety Advisor
- Safety Advisor is a policeman not a coach, or
- Safety Advisor concentrates on bureaucratic process rather than behaviours.

Competence of workers
- Faith placed in a 'ticket' rather than testing, monitoring and giving feedback to a new worker, or
- Your behavioural safety practices are not rolled out to your supply chain.

Reports
- Reports are only produced to satisfy the directors, or
- Reports are so convoluted and full of dismembered statistics that your staff and workforce would never find them of value.

Injury and incident investigations
- Investigation done by the Safety advisor not the supervisors, or
- The report does not identify the pinpointed behaviours that lead to the incident or
- The report may be badly composed and the end result is a safety alert that will have no lasting effect in prevention.

Procurement of the supply chain
- Procurement exercise is a paper based questionnaire, or
- No consequence for poor performance/ performance not measured and recorded or used for further selection.

Director's interventions
- Letting your director believe that by doing a safety tour he/she is leading safety, or
- Not coaching your director in how to 'behave' when he/she receives bad news.

1.16 - Leadership behaviours

Most people can relate to worker behaviours quite easily. The worker is or isn't behaving in a safe manner, which we can all observe and agree upon. On the other hand, it's more difficult to deal with the safe or unsafe behaviour of the leaders and other managers involved in the project.

This list has been put together to help people decide what to observe in themselves and others which may help them be pinpointed, allow for feedback and ultimately help improve behaviour.

Communication

Always ask "Can you show me how this will impact on safety?" Be calm.
* Well run companies run on confidence; don't do anything which gives the impression of panic.

Coaching not emailing.
* Coaching is the most effective way of engaging people in the business. Email is the least effective way of engaging people in the business.

Be a role model in your communications and actions. Think what message you are going to send out
* Leaders need to be reliable, reply to emails, phone calls, turn up on time, complete actions, finish on time, this will engender trust, and others will see this and copy it. Leaders are role-models, yes, you are a role model.

"Do this by this date but do it safely" is different from "Do this safely but do it by this date!"

Planning

Plan well and hire competent people.
* High levels of safety performance come from well planned jobs which are competently staffed. It is the leaders' job to create an environment where good planning occurs and where good people are hired and developed.

Ensure competent foremen are hired.
- The route to improved safety on sites is concentrated at the foreman level. Competent foremen are the key, and leaders need to create environments which hire and train competent foremen.
- Foremen should understand behaviour change, pinpointing and feedback.

Plan frequent safety inspections.
- Traditional safety inspections measure results on sites at the time of the inspections. Re-evaluating inspection and auditing behaviours will lead to more useful measures, which can in turn affect safety improvements.

Put dead time in your diary.
- Making yourself too busy is destructive, it gives the impression you are not in control. It's very important to put dead time in your diary which will be taken up by the inevitable urgent demands on your time. Measure how much dead time needs to be there. This time can then be used to deal with emergencies or follow up coaching with your identified safety leaders.

Performance Measurement

Regularly evaluate staff performance
- Leaders should check that their staff are competent, using objective and frequent measures.

Determine what controls the current safety performance.
- Leaders should learn what natural reinforcers exist in their company environment. It may be depressing but a better view of the reality of the company will inevitably lead to better business (and safety) decisions.

Set goals.
- Leaders should help safety professionals find a useful positive role in the business, not just safety. Setting improvement goals for them will change their direction. Safety advisors must feel they are part of the decision making team.

Provide public feedback.
- Leaders should solicit feedback and publish measurements on their own critical behaviours. They need to demonstrate that they are serious about this and also experience for themselves what they are asking others to do.
- Safety advisors should help leaders with a variety of surveys such as climate surveys, anonymous surveys, web based surveys, digital pen surveys.
- Safety advisors should be analysing the data from surveys and making compelling cases for what the data shows.

Provide specific reinforcement.
- Leaders should make their R+ contingent on something they observed, make it specific and it will be very powerful. Platitudes do nothing but irritate the troops.

Focusing on Safety

Create an environment that supports safety.
- Bid managers and some other senior managers will be under so much pressure to win jobs where safety will suffer, leaders must set up the environment where this is recognised.
- Lump sum jobs should have the same monetary value on safety as cost reimbursable ones; leaders can ask if this is the case and ask for evidence.

Don't give up on safety.
- Safety issues need to be challenged, always. Do not allow people to use the law as an excuse for a complicated process; they simply didn't make enough time to write a simple process.

Trust your employees.
- Self-auditing is possible, with imagination you can use more of this. Leaders should make this point, it says, "I trust you".

Set up an environment supportive of behavioural safety.
- Leaders should control the threat of something new in the environment, or people's energy will be on killing it. Align reinforcement for this new initiative and the behaviours that support it.

Be consistent.
- Leaders should have a consistent approach. Being behaviourally sound about one particular issue, then reverting to type over others will just confuse people and erode trust.

1.17 Safety professionals and behavioural safety

The safety fraternity is made up of professionals who are qualified in safety competencies and usually have a good idea of what the law requires everyone to do. They usually find themselves trying to enforce regulations whilst providing senior managers with reports, responses and reassurance of compliance.

Some safety professionals are enlightened to behavioural safety and play more of an educational and coaching role. Safety professionals that are exposed to behavioural science sometimes find it difficult to wrestle themselves out of their own world of paperwork and compliance.

Those who have managed to break free have become great advocates of behavioural methods and have discovered the benefits of observing, measuring and analysing before acting. They are also implementing sensible processes and procedures.

It is important to understand why some health and safety procedures may be received as punishment and once this is recognised, how behavioural methods can be used to develop a rewarding regime.

We all need to be aware that every employee or worker has a primary consequence provider they will take notice of. This is a powerful lesson to those that try to influence the behaviour of total strangers whilst visiting a site. Safety Advisors who influence and coach the site agent and foreman have a much bigger impact on safety, than those who try to influence the worker directly.

Safety Advisors that simply police and always pick fault will have little impact on the safety culture of the company.

> **" This volume of safety paperwork creates unsafe situations on sites. "**

In any organisation the quality of the antecedents in play will have a big impact on the effectiveness of performance. In most companies there are a plethora of safety antecedents, many volumes of them, lots designed to cover the company in case of threat of prosecution.

This volume of safety paperwork creates unsafe situations on sites. The safety processes spawn many form filling exercises and many of these are usually designed to catch every eventuality, legally. This creates a belief that the management of health and safety is good because a bit of paper has been filled out. The behaviour of filling the form in becomes important, not the behaviour of working safely and creating a safe environment.

Behaviourally speaking most humans have a limit on what they could and will read, also they have a limit on how many forms they will fill in, no matter what the threats are. The local environment will dictate their behaviour.

The dilemma here is to create a safe set of processes which take into account the behavioural limitations on all the performers, staying within the law and creating safe behaviours – not just ticking forms. It's not impossible, many people achieve this in other areas of law and many achieve this on the subject of safety.

Here are some helpful hints on how to achieve a workable and legal set of safety processes and how you can engage the safety professionals:-

1. Make sure behavioural safety is integrated into company safety procedures. Pinpoint the behaviours you want the procedure to create – does it create them?
2. Reduce company safety documentation to a lean state.
   a. Analyse which parts of current safety processes are actually tied to legislation and why. Challenge myth and legend.
   b. Look to change wordy documentation to flow charts.
   c. Have a % reduction/year measure on paperwork safety processes.
3. Analyse safety data (hazards, injuries etc) to focus efforts toward the right areas.
4. Develop meaningful lead indicators.
5. Inspect sites, arrange for staff to inspect in rotation.
   a. Focus inspections on what the supervisor does.
   b. Ask workers for feedback on safety.
   c. Ask questions on verbal safety communication.
6. Champion the removal of barriers to safety.
   a. Ask "What prevents you working safely, and what pushes you to cut corners?"
7. Set up a feedback system from the business to the Safety department for their improvement.
8. Simplify audits so that the performer could carry them out and get the same score as the Safety Auditor thereby illustrating it's objective and ensuring the expectations are clear; create an inspection that can achieve 100%.
9. Safety advisors should clearly identify to sites what is necessary for legal compliance, what is virtual safety and expand on real safety activity.
   a. Produce a plan to expand real safety and remove virtual safety.
   b. Work to remove bureaucracy in site documentation at all levels.

Questions you can ask safety advisors to get an early read on their climate:-

1. What proportion of your time is spent reporting?
2. What are the obstacles stopping your performance improving within your company?
3. What feedback do you receive from the business on your performance?
4. Who is your customer?
5. What is the most satisfying element within your current role?
6. What is your biggest frustration in your current role?
7. What does a great Safety Department look like?

By maintaining a voluminous and bureaucratic health and safety system that is not fully useable you are reinforcing the fact that Safety is a bolt on. You have created a virtual system, disparate from the reality of your business.

1.18 Some case studies

Safety incident story, in a town near you.....

I was standing outside our local convenience store which was being renovated and I noticed a man struggling to fix a facia plate on the side of the roof of the building. He was standing on a filled up wheeled cardboard container and it was wobbling a bit.

> " if leaders create the right environment then site managers and supervisors will indeed engage in improving site safety:- "

He got off the container and asked his supervisor if they could get a platform for him to complete the work safely as it was indeed a bit precarious. The supervisor said, "Oh yeah, I'm going to order you a platform and delay this job by one day just so you can have an easier time. Get up there and get it done now."

Of course the guy climbed back onto his wheeled cardboard bin and finished the job. There it was before my very eyes, the classic helpless and distressed guy working for a tyrannical boss. I looked at the worker, he looked sheepish. I looked at the supervisor, he looked sheepish as well.

The situation above is common, I have observed many similar situations, I could have intervened but that would have caused me stress and would have set both the other parties against me. It would have been as much use as clapping one's hands once a day to scare the birds away from your newly seeded lawn.

We have received many case studies from the attendees of our behavioural safety courses. Here are three of them. They demonstrate that if leaders create the right environment then site managers and supervisors will indeed engage in improving site safety:-

Using behavioural safety to encourage close call data.

The foreman shared the current close call data with the rest of the site staff at their management team meeting. The team decided that they were not making the best use of the information which must be available on the site regarding hazard spotting and close calls. They decided they would increase their enquiries of the workforce regarding hazards and close calls.

For 5 minutes at the start of the next few shift briefings, the foreman enquired about any hazards or close calls observed by the workers the previous day. The information gained on hazards increased by some 350% over a period of 3 weeks. Close calls proved a little bit more difficult to tease out of the workers but over the next few months a number of important safety improvements were implemented following discussions on close calls between the foremen and workers at start shift briefings.

Using behavioural safety to make work easier.

A foreman on one of our safety courses informed us that when he took over from the previous site foreman he had the opportunity to change a number of things making the site tidier and a better place to work. The first thing he did was to look where people were walking between different areas on the site and moved the designated walkways to where people were actually walking (where he could).

The same thing applies to paperwork, procedures, forms; why not carry out a 'how much of our current processes do we really need' exercise? What about a target reduction in voluminous & dispiriting paperwork? A reduction in the number of meetings, reports down to a level which actually adds value; a kind of paperwork version of 'putting the designated walkway in the place people want to walk'.

Using behavioural safety to create and deliver good toolbox talks

A foreman went on one of our behavioural safety courses, and was asked to gather data on an issue he wanted to improve. For some time he'd felt frustrated with the tool box talks that were delivered to the team as he felt they weren't getting across the important message he wanted to communicate. Additionally, when he reviewed the data, he found that 80% of incidents were due to routine work, exactly the type of work that was discussed at the tool box talks.

The foreman met with his supervisors that delivered the tool box talks. He asked for their feedback on what he could do to improve them. They said that the information was too complex, too long to fit into a short TBT and often based on suggestions from head office, not what was relevant to current activities on site.

The foreman decided to see if he could simplify the TBT's. For each TBT he set a limit of 5 key bullet points, and if possible drew a simple picture to help illustrate his point. He also prepared a few questions that the supervisor could ask the operatives to check that he'd got his point across.

The supervisors rolled out the new style TBT's; after a few months when the foreman reviewed the data, he found that minor injuries/first aid cases had reduced from one every 2 days to one every 12 days.

1.19 Summary

- Local workplace environment drives behaviour.
- Management creates this environment for workers.
- Leadership creates the environment for the Management.
- Behavioural science will help to make the improvements required in all these different environments.

Appendix 1

Introduction to the BMT Federation

Behavioural Management Techniques (BMT) is the phrase used to describe the use of applied behaviour analysis for the improvement of business and safety performance.

The Federation mission is to facilitate partnering for the dissemination of BMT within businesses and projects.

Purpose of the Federation

The purpose of the Federation is to allow current Clients of the BMT Federation access to a wider population of similar practitioners who are engaged in applying BMT to improve their business and safety performance.

BMT conferences

For the last seven years the Federation has organised a major BMT conference normally held in the spring, and for the last five years a Behavioural Safety conference has been held in the autumn. The conferences provide an opportunity for speakers to present papers on their successes with BMT and safety.

There is usually a mix of keynote speeches from guest speakers, our Clients and from the Federation members. There is always opportunity for discussion on a wide range of related BMT and safety topics.

For more information, log on to www.bmtfed.com.

Appendix 2

Other Hollin books publications

HOW TO EMPTY THE TOO HARD BOX - *By Howard Lees*
ISBN number 978-0-9563114-4-3 - £6.50

BEHAVIOURAL COACHING (2nd edition) - *By Howard Lees*
ISBN number 978-0-9563114-2-9 - £6.50

HOW TO ESCAPE FROM CLOUD CUCKOO LAND - *By Howard Lees*
ISBN number 978-0-9563114-0-5 - £6.50

NOTES ON BEHAVIOURAL MANAGEMENT TECHNIQUES - *By Howard Lees*
ISBN number 978-0-9563114-1-2 - £6.50

IDEAS FOR WIMPS - *By Howard Lees*
ISBN number 978-0-9563114-6-7 - £12.00

notes: